The National WWII
Museum

The New Orleans
Train Garden

Faulkner House Books

ON THE LOOSE
IN NEW ORLEANS

Dear Animal Detectives,

The animals included in this book are ones I thought you would recognize and have fun finding (at least in these pages) on the streets of New Orleans. Many of them can be found at the Audubon Zoo, which currently houses 360 different species, including many that are rare or endangered. For more information, visit www.audubonnatureinstitute.org. Or, better yet, visit the zoo in person.

P.S. In real life the zoo does an excellent job making sure its animals are happy at home and don't go wandering off!

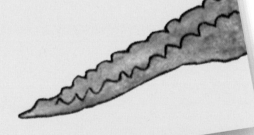

ON THE LOOSE
IN NEW ORLEANS

A Find-the-Animals Book

Written and Illustrated
by Sage Stossel

arcadia®
CHILDREN'S BOOKS

FOR
MIKE AND KIERAN

ISBN 978-1-4671-9716-8

Series design by John Barnett/4 Eyes Design

Published by Arcadia Children's Books
A Division of Arcadia Publishing, Inc
Charleston, SC

Visit us at www.arcadiapublishing.com

Visit Sage Stossel at www.sagestossel.com

Printed in China

In the bustling Big Easy,
In Audubon Park,
Lies a wonderful zoo
That closes at dark.

One morning the keeper
discovered a note:
"We've gone for a walk,"
the animals wrote.

"Oh dear," said the keeper
"What am I to do?
My critters have left me
alone at the zoo!"

The cages, indeed, were all empty that day,
for the creatures, it seemed, had meandered away.

1 tiger, 1 alligator, 5 monkeys, 1 elephant, 1 lion, 1 sea lion, 1 emu, 2 snakes, 1 bear, and 1 turtle?
(Do you also see several lifelike elephant and lion statues
on the rocks in the center of the fountain?)

CAN YOU FIND

Then word came from Canal Street that "Something's not right:
The streetcars have filled up with riders that bite!"

1 giraffe, 2 elephants, 2 sea lions, 1 anteater, 1 rhino, 2 emus,
3 snakes, 1 alligator, 1 lion, 1 flamingo, 2 monkeys, and 2 bears?

CAN
YOU
FIND

café du monde

A report came in next from the town's famed café:
"There are elephants here, eating up our beignets!"

4 elephants, 1 snake, 3 monkeys, 1 anteater, 1 pelican, 1 tiger, 1 bear,
2 turtles, 1 giraffe, 1 lion, 1 emu, 1 sea lion, 2 alligators, and 1 rhino?

CAN YOU FIND

Meanwhile, out in the bayou, a sightseeing tour
was surprised by a lion, who just said, "Bonjour."

1 lion, 2 giraffes, 3 alligators, 2 rhinos, 1 sloth, 2 sea lions,
1 bear, 1 anteater, 1 parrot, 1 tiger, 1 pelican, 3 snakes,
2 turtles, 1 elephant, 1 emu, 2 monkeys, and 1 egret?

CAN
YOU
FIND

The scene got quite lively around Jackson Square
as a bevy of animals frolicked with flair.

2 bears, 2 alligators, 1 giraffe, 2 emus, 1 monkey, 1 anteater, 1 rhino, 2 turtles, 3 snakes, and 1 lion?

CAN YOU FIND

Riverboats cruised merrily on
as a jazz-loving tiger sang notes that were wrong.

2 tigers, 1 rhino, 4 snakes, 2 sea lions, 1 turtle, 2 elephants, 1 zebra, 2 bears,
1 flamingo, 2 alligators, 3 monkeys, 2 emus, 2 lions, and 2 giraffes?

CAN
YOU
FIND

At the old State Museum, the crowds were quite stirred
both by fabulous costumes—and show-stealing birds.

1 peacock, 1 emu, 2 alligators, 1 bear, 1 rhino, 1 lion, 2 snakes,
2 monkeys, 1 elephant, 2 tigers, and 1 turtle?

CAN YOU FIND

Hot parties were hopping on hip Bourbon Street
as humans and animals bopped to the beat.

1 tiger, 1 rhino, 2 snakes, 1 elephant, 1 bear, 1 monkey,
2 lions, 1 alligator, 2 emus, and 1 sea lion?

CAN YOU FIND

Louis Armstrong's great park was soon rocking with sound
as a band played his music, and creatures flocked 'round.

1 lion, 2 bears, 2 tigers, 1 alligator, 2 giraffes, 1 turtle,
2 snakes, 2 emus, 1 anteater, and 2 elephants?

The aquarium staff weren't quite sure what to do
when a deep-diving monkey joined up with their krewe.

1 monkey, 2 alligators, 1 anteater, 1 lizard, 1 rhino, 1 turtle, 1 giraffe, 1 lemur, 3 snakes, 1 emu, and 1 flamingo?

CAN YOU FIND

Then the grand Garden District got lively quite fast
as cute creatures arrived, each one having a blast.

1 giraffe, 1 lion, 2 emus, 1 rhino, 2 alligators, 1 bear, 1 parrot,
2 monkeys, 1 anteater, 2 snakes, 1 turtle, and 1 elephant?

CAN YOU FIND

When at last night descended,
The zookeeper smiled,
as back through the gate
all his animals filed.

What a wonderful day
they appeared to have had,
but to be back at home
they seemed equally glad.

As for where they had been,
they refused to confess,
but the keeper was smart
and could probably guess.

Can you help these animals find their way home to the zoo?

Also available in this series...

More online...

Visit www.OnTheLooseinNewOrleans.com
for New Orleans pictures to print
and color, ideas for things to do
around the city, and more.

SAGE STOSSEL is an editor and cartoonist who regularly cartoons for the *Boston Globe* and the *Provincetown Banner*. She is the recipient of the award for Best Editorial Cartoon by the National Society of Newspaper Columnists, and a New England Press Association Award. Her cartoons have been featured by the *New York Times*, *The Washington Post*, *Politico*, *CNN Headline News*, and *Best Editorial Cartoons of the Year*. Her books include *On the Loose in Boston*, *On the Loose in Washington, DC.*, *On the Loose in Philadelphia*, *On the Loose in New York City*, the graphic novel *Starling*, and *T-Ride*, a board book about riding the Boston subway.

www.sagestossel.com

Louisiana Children's Museum

Audubon Butterfly Garden & Insectarium

Lafayette Cemetery

Commander's Palace